Self-Esteem

A Comprehensive Handbook For Overcoming Low Self-esteem And Resolving Internal Conflicts To Restore And Enhance Personal Confidence

(Thorough Guidance For Improving Self-assurance And Unleashing Your Maximum Potential)

Rayford Hodges

TABLE OF CONTENT

Alter The Ways In Which You Think. 1

Emotional Intelligence 30

Why Do Goals Fail To Produce Desired Outcomes For The Majority Of Individuals? 39

Do Not Entertain Unwarranted Negative Remarks. 55

What Is This? 68

Fundamental Tenets Of Objective Establishment 108

Do Something That Brings You Joy. 120

Alter The Ways In Which You Think.

The intriguing aspect regarding individuals' perception of reality lies in the fact that, oftentimes, their perception is merely an outcome of their cognitive routines. If you consistently analyze situations with a pessimistic mindset, it becomes effortless for you to draw the conclusion that this is the sole manner in which individuals can interpret these signals. This is the only form of justice they are entitled to. In light of the circumstances, given that you tend to interpret situations as they are based on specific feedback or stimuli, one can conclude that it represents a factual state of affairs. It is possible that your perspective aligns with this belief due to its habitual nature. Your cognitive processes are structured in a manner that invariably leads you to a specific outcome.

What would the outcome be if you were to alter your cognitive routines? If you were to alter your cognitive frameworks, what would occur? Does this imply that you would invariably arrive at identical assessments? There is a significant likelihood that your perception of self-worth and personal value will undergo a transformation upon the alteration of your mental patterns.

It is imperative to understand that mental habits are consciously selected. I am aware that this statement may appear unconventional, as one might be inclined to argue that it is solely a result of their natural birth circumstances. This is simply a reflection of my personal sentiment. Perhaps it would be advisable for you to reconsider, as the manner in which you interpret your perception of reality must have originated from a particular source. It is an acquired knowledge or skill that you have obtained through your experiences. The majority of individuals acquire their cognitive patterns from their parental figures. Furthermore, we acquire this knowledge through regular association and companionship with individuals. The existence of groupthink is an undeniable reality. By altering your social circle, you would likely witness a notable transformation in your cognitive patterns and demeanor.

Nevertheless, it is imperative that you scrutinize your cognitive patterns. It is a decision that one makes. It is not an innate quality. It is not an imposition beyond your control, devoid of any autonomy or alternative. You consistently possess the capability to exercise your freedom of choice. You can remain aware of your cognitive patterns and actively resist them.

Be committed

Nevertheless, it is possible that your insufficient self-confidence has placed you at a disadvantage in the context of delivering oral presentations. We will classify this characteristic as a vulnerability of yours. Your organizational abilities are commendable; however, your proficiency in report preparation is exemplary, and the boss has already conveyed satisfaction with your expertise. You possess a colleague who exhibits exceptional public speaking skills, as well as another who has attained mastery in the domain of organization.

Public speaking may not be suitable for everyone. Lamenting your ineptitude to confidently address an audience with the same ease as engaging in friendly conversation serves no purpose. It is possible to make slight improvements in this area, however, without possessing the inherent ability to communicate effectively in public, one may never truly achieve the level of finesse expected in public speaking. This does not imply that you are incapable of and undeserving of the promotion. Seek advice from your colleague and observe their actions for potential guidance. Kindly request the assistance of your colleague in organizing and decluttering your work area. This will foster a sense of worth and dignity in them, while also providing an opportunity to glean valuable insights from individuals possessing diverse skill sets.

One can make a favorable impression on their superior by consistently demonstrating punctuality and consistently producing exceptional reports. Direct some of your focus towards refining your organisational skills, while devoting the majority of your efforts towards enhancing the quality of your statements. That is your area of expertise, and that is what will propel you to a higher position.

7

Self-Improvement through motivation

Alleviating concerns to foster an optimistic perspective

Fears and phobias can have an impact on individuals to some extent, whereas the

The majority of individuals can overcome their fear, and the vast majority of fear and phobias are regarded with disdain.

Beyond mere apprehensions, fear and phobia could pose significant distress and upheaval to certain individuals.

Significantly impacts their day-to-day existence.

Fear and phobias unequivocally elicit pessimism, while consistent antagonism can be demoralizing, whereas a small number of

Fears and dread can be deeply rooted, but they can gradually be overcome with the passage of time and persistence.

help. There exist various approaches to provide assistance, and the more deeply ingrained the dread or apprehension,

It is likely that expert guidance pertaining to a cure could be well-informed in the framework.

ment or hypnotherapy. In the event that the apprehension is of a mild nature, it may be surmounted through the utilization of self-improvement techniques.

Understanding fear and phobias

In order to overcome fears and phobias, it is imperative that one comprehends them fully, apprehension.

Phobia effectively induces uncomfortable contemplations and emotions when exposed to particular circumstances.

stances. It can lead to various symptoms such as illness, nausea, dizziness, and discomfort.

Sensation, a constricted pressure around the cranium, discomfort in the thoracic region, a feeling of breathlessness and quivering. These are generally considered emotions that we allow ourselves to experience.

Attaining mastery over our cognitive and physical faculties, dispelling apprehension entails reclaiming

Exerting influence and establishing perspective.

This concept forms the basis for the restoration of fear or phobia, notwithstanding the fact that it is not widely recognized.

Considering the extensive period during which you have experienced a decline, it is expected that your recovery process will require a significant amount of time.

peration is conceivable. Fears and phobias can essentially be characterized as misrepresented feelings of unease, and

Acquiring knowledge about various relaxation methods and strategies provides a solid foundation for alleviating phobias and anxieties.

There exists a wide array of self-enhancement materials ranging from instructional manuals, DVDs, courses, and audio programs which have the potential to serve as

Assist you in initiating a process, any instructional resources designed for effectively handling discomfort.

Determination and resilience are essential, albeit there exist numerous resources specifically tailored to individuals with phobia and fear.

1: Techniques for safeguarding oneself against energy vampires

Gain Awareness and Safeguard Against Individuals who Deplete Your Energy Reserves

Energy vampires are individuals who possess the ability to deplete a substantial amount of vitality from one's being. They consistently encounter a multitude of challenges and frequently approach you, seeking an excessive level of assistance beyond reasonable expectations. As an individual with empathetic abilities, one senses and comprehends the perspectives of others, genuinely empathizes with them, and assumes a personal duty to supply them with the necessary vitality to fulfill their requirements. This situation rapidly transforms into a perpetual cycle, wherein you find yourself constantly exerting efforts to cater to the energy requirements of the individual, yet remain unable to fully satisfy their needs. This is due to the fact that they exhibit characteristics of an energy vampire.

To safeguard oneself from individuals who drain energy, it is essential to acquire the ability to assertively decline requests. Developing the skill of declining and firmly upholding one's decision holds significant significance. Herein lies a method to fortify your sense of self-assurance and security in asserting your refusal. When declining the request of an individual who drains your energy, it is imperative to actively and intentionally refuse both verbally and energetically. Certain individuals may envisage their defensive barrier effectively obstructing the solicitation, thus impeding the influx of energy into their personal realm entirely. It is crucial to prevent the influx of energy from the energy vampire. If you allow its influence, it has the capability to instigate empathetic responses within you that may induce a shift in your perspective. This concern diminishes as one becomes more proficient in safeguarding oneself; however, during the initial stages, one is vulnerable to altering one's perspective due to the influence of this energetic force.

In order to safeguard yourself from assuming additional responsibilities, it will be necessary to identify individuals who drain your energy and acquire the skill of refusing their demands. It is essential to acknowledge and reinforce the notion that one should not be obligated to meet the needs of others beyond what is deemed reasonable. If your actions are not motivated by genuine affection for both yourself and the other individual, then they are not aligned with the intended recipient's best interests. If one engages in an activity that demands an undue amount of energy beyond one's reasonable capacity, it can be concluded that an excessive level of commitment is being displayed. It is imperative to ensure that you acquire the necessary knowledge on effectively declining requests and purposefully purging your energy field of such appeals. This will provide you with safeguards against the negative influence of excessive energy, unwarranted requests, and individuals who drain others' energy levels. Additionally, it is advisable to reduce the duration of your interactions with the energy vampire as much as feasible and implement more assertive boundary-setting measures regarding the topics you are willing to engage with them on. This will contribute significantly to establishing a heightened level of defense against the energy vampire. By adopting this approach, you can avoid the perpetual state of defensiveness and allow yourself the freedom to relax and derive pleasure from life.

Guard yourself against time predators as well

Furthermore, apart from individuals who drain energy, there also exist individuals who consume significant amounts of time. Often, an energy vampire may also be characterized as a time vampire. Nevertheless, it must be acknowledged that not all individuals who consume excessive amounts of time can be classified as energy vampires. Time vampires refer to individuals who excessively consume a significant portion of your valuable time. One may frequently find oneself engaged in activities on their behalf, dedicating an excessive amount of time to their presence, or investing a significant portion of one's time in concern for their well-being. Consequently, they ultimately consume a disproportionate amount of your valuable time.

The most effective approach to addressing a time-consuming individual is to establish boundaries and restrict the amount of time you are willing to allocate to them. Establish the necessary boundaries for yourself, commit to them, and remain steadfast in upholding them. Commence reinforcing this behavior by strictly adhering to the allocated time frame and firmly declining any requests that surpass the set limit. This equally applies when you contemplate their significance. In the event that you experience concerns regarding the individual, exercise self-restraint and establish personal limits accordingly. Limiting the duration of your interactions with an individual, particularly someone who exhibits toxic behaviors towards you, can effectively bolster your well-being and fortify your personal security.

While it is indeed commendable to assist individuals and foster their well-being, it should be noted that it is not incumbent upon you to assume this responsibility. Engage in a sincere introspection regarding the reasons underlying your sense of personal responsibility towards others, and subsequently establish firm boundaries for yourself as well. Establishing these personal boundaries will facilitate your ability to avoid assuming personal responsibility for the needs and emotions of others. Subsequently, it will enhance your ability to decline and safeguard your precious time. When declining, ensure that you allocate that period for engaging in a meaningful practice of self-care. The better you prioritize self-care, the more evident it becomes that you are deserving of your own time, energy, and focus to a greater extent than anyone else. Despite any initial sense of unease or perceived lack of alignment with your personal inclinations. In due course, you will come to comprehend that it is an essential measure for safeguarding oneself and maintaining personal well-being. In addition to promoting a heightened sense of well-being, it will also enhance your capacity to offer assistance to others.

5.1 Exercises

The initial exercise we shall discuss pertains to the subject of journaling. Engaging in the practice of journaling offers a valuable opportunity for individuals seeking to enhance their emotional intelligence. This activity involves the act of externalizing one's thoughts, thereby enabling a more objective exploration of the intricate elements of one's psyche. Engaging in the act of recording one's thoughts and experiences, regardless of their seemingly ordinary nature, can evoke a sense of satisfaction and provide valuable insights into one's daily life, as well as future aspirations. The practice of journaling can be effortlessly incorporated into one's routine, devoid of any arduousness or perceived retribution. It is advisable to begin the practice of journaling in a gradual and cautious manner. It would be advisable to consider purchasing a designated notebook for this specific purpose. Some people enjoy typing. If one desires to engage in a distinctive tactile ambiance and explore their creative faculties, acquiring a typewriter designated for journaling purposes would be an apt recommendation.

Please feel free to explore various approaches in order to enhance your level of interest and engagement. Commence by recording intricate particulars of your day, subsequently progressing towards documenting a greater level of detail. One can investigate specific dates wherein emotional experiences are encountered. Initially, endeavor to separate and articulate the subjective emotional encounter. Make an effort to recollect the bodily and mental state you were experiencing, endeavoring to mentally reconstruct the circumstances. Sensing the bodily sensations under these circumstances can effectively trigger the emotional reaction within oneself, thereby enabling its monitoring and observation.

After performing this action several times, you can review the notes from each emotional encounter and determine if your findings are congruent. Did you experience similar physiological sensations in your body on Tuesday, the 11th, as you did during your previous episode of anger? What were the cognitive elements accompanying each emotional encounter, and to what extent did they align? You may discover compelling data and information within this resource that will foster a heightened understanding of your emotional experiences.

Individuals will have unique and distinctive emotional experiences, and this diversity is beneficial and essential. Certain individuals may shed tears in moments of sadness, while others may experience feelings of anger. Certain individuals exhibit a greater sense of ease towards certain emotions as compared to others. One illustration of this can be seen in individuals who find solace in being characterized as an indignant individual, as their extensive past encounters have molded them into such. They have been exposed to individuals who readily exhibit their anger, and as a result, they have also acquired the tendency to readily express their anger. With regards to feelings of sorrow, though, they possess no understanding or ability to adequately convey or exhibit it. They may even experience a sense of shame in exhibiting their sorrow. Certain demographic cohorts exhibit a propensity to align with either one or the other.

An alternative approach to cultivating emotional intelligence is through engaging in introspection. Once more, endeavor to approach this task in a manner that suits your comfort. Should you have an inclination towards spending time amidst natural surroundings, I would recommend paying a visit to your preferred nature park. There, you may find solace in an instance of tranquility, allowing for introspection upon a recent emotional disposition experienced by yourself. It would also be advisable to direct your focus towards your present emotional condition and inquire: "What is my current emotional state?" "What is the root cause behind my current emotional state?" By examining the past experiences that have contributed to your present state, you can discern effective approaches to enhance or prevent such emotional outbursts.

Next, we will proceed to examine the second exercise, which involves the development or repetition of positive affirmations. These concise affirmations hold the potential to induce a greater sense of positivity and relaxation when attended to or recited.

Presented below are a selection of positive affirmations as illustrations:

I possess the ability to accomplish various tasks.

I am prepared to exert my utmost effort.

I will engage in the noble struggle.

I possess the knowledge and determination to persevere and not succumb to discouragement.

I possess the knowledge and ability to attain my desired objectives.

Individuals do not harbor malicious intentions towards me. Rather, their primary focus is directed towards the pursuit of their own lives.

I possess command over my actions for the day.

My contemplations are purely mental.

One's thoughts do not determine one's essence.

I possess a greater amount of power than I currently perceive.

I am grateful for the beauty that permeates my life, despite the trials I have overcome to reach this point.

I am an individual who warrants both respect and the attainment of success.

I am an autonomous individual.

I possess cognitive capacity, fortitude, and intellectual acuity.

I deserve to receive affection and love.

I am entitled to the same rights and privileges as any other individual.

I am a warrior.

I can do this.

I am present today, and my presence will endure through tomorrow.

I am valid.

I have a place.

I am fortunate to have individuals in my life who have a genuine concern for my well-being.

I possess genuine concern for the well-being of others.

My life matters.

My life is important.

All individuals' emotions hold intrinsic value, regardless of their nature. Individuals who have developed a sense of inferiority during their upbringing will need to alter those beliefs in order to gain confidence in their instincts and confront their surroundings with sound discernment. One potential approach to address this matter is by implementing exposure therapy. As previously indicated, the fundamental tenets of exposure therapy revolve around the notion of engaging in activities that elicit discomfort or unease. By subjecting oneself to a protracted engagement with an action or circumstance that elicits anxiety or unease, one can gradually acclimate and develop an increased tolerance for said action or circumstance over time. One will progressively acquire the ability to handle it more effectively and endure its perceived adverse effects by becoming more adept at handling pressure. If one's self-assurance is lacking, particularly in specific scenarios, it is advisable to gradually expose oneself to such situations in order to develop resilience and cultivate a positive reaction towards what was previously considered embarrassing. Put simply, venture outside of your familiar environment.

Emotional Intelligence

In the preceding chapter, we provided a concise overview of emotional intelligence and its status as a highly coveted attribute among employers. The concept of emotional intelligence was coined by Peter Salavoy and John Mayer, distinguished scholars who made significant contributions to the study of this subject. Currently, the definition of emotional intelligence pertains to an individual's capacity to acknowledge, comprehend, and regulate their emotional state. It may also be characterized as an individual's capacity to perceive, comprehend, and exert influence over the emotional states of others. Put simply, emotional intelligence (EI) is the capacity to recognize that emotions guide human actions and possess the potential to influence others. By acquiring the skill of emotional management, one can effectively influence oneself and others in a beneficial manner.

Emotional intelligence comprises the subsequent five constituents:

● Personal introspection: By possessing a heightened level of personal introspection, individuals can discern their own aptitudes and limitations, allowing them to navigate and respond appropriately to various situations and people.

● Emotional self-control: Individuals with a high degree of emotional intelligence exhibit the ability to effectively regulate their emotions and exercise self-control when necessary.

● Determ

● Empathy: Individuals who possess a strong sense of empathy and compassion tend to achieve greater levels of success in establishing connections with others.

● Social competence: An individual with elevated emotional intelligence possesses the social aptitude to effectively demonstrate their regard and consideration for others. This is the reason individuals with elevated emotional intelligence often exhibit greater compatibility with a wide range of individuals.

Notwithstanding the criticism, emotional intelligence is a concept that profoundly resonates with the broader populace. This topic holds greater allure within specific industries." "There is heightened attraction towards this topic in select industries." "This topic garners increased interest in particular sectors. In recent times, a significant number of organizations have integrated personality assessments into their employment screening procedures with the intent of discerning individuals possessing elevated emotional intelligence (EI), as it is suggestive of their potential as superior team members or leaders.

The Significance of Emotional Intelligence

Over the years, the significance of emotional intelligence has significantly escalated, particularly in the context of professional environments. Merely entering one's workplace does not entail an automatic cessation of emotional experiences that were present prior to arrival. Despite the common perception, emotions are consistently present in the workplace, albeit typically controlled to maintain a professional demeanor. Many individuals frequently adopt a façade of emotional detachment during work hours in order to maintain a professional demeanor.

In contemporary society, the significance of emotional intelligence cannot be overstated, primarily due to the distinctive nature of workplace culture. Currently, the prevailing norm is that a considerable majority of tasks are accomplished through collective efforts as opposed to individual endeavors. Progressive employers understand that acknowledging emotions in the workplace fosters the creation of more conducive working environments. This implies that individuals should exercise greater mindfulness and consideration towards both their own emotions and those of others. Individuals with higher levels of emotional intelligence exhibit greater flexibility in response to change, a crucial aptitude in contemporary, rapidly evolving circumstances.

Workplace leaders who possess higher levels of emotional intelligence tend to cultivate greater employee satisfaction, resulting in reduced expenses associated with employee turnover and enhanced overall efficiency within the workplace. As previously addressed, individuals with elevated emotional intelligence commonly experience greater life satisfaction in non-professional settings, as they exhibit a reduced susceptibility to disorders such as depression and anxiety.

Outlined below are several approaches that individuals can employ to enhance their emotional intelligence:

● Contemplate your emotions: Engaging in introspection regarding one's emotions fosters the development of self-awareness. To cultivate one's emotional intelligence, it is imperative to begin by reflecting upon one's own emotions and the manner in which they are expressed during adverse circumstances. Once you enhance your level of awareness regarding the emotions you are experiencing, you can commence the process of effectively managing and regulating them.

● Seek an alternative viewpoint: Individuals' interpretations of reality may vary. Commence by soliciting the viewpoints of others and endeavor to comprehend your demeanor in circumstances rife with emotional intensity.

● Take note: Following the onset of enhanced self-awareness, endeavor to attain a more comprehensive comprehension of your conduct. Commence the act of observing your emotions and directing your focus towards them.

● Take a momentary pause: Cease your actions momentarily to contemplate and discern the emotions that you experience. Engaging in this behavior might prove challenging during instances when emotions are running high, yet with regular practice, it will eventually become ingrained.

● Enhance empathy by gaining an understanding of the underlying reasons behind an individual's emotional state or feelings. Make an effort to empathize and visualize the perspective of others, contemplating how it would feel to be in their position.

● Opted to derive lessons from constructive feedback: Undoubtedly, the reception of criticism may not be preferred by most individuals, yet it remains an unavoidable facet of existence. Elect to derive lessons from criticism rather than immediately embracing a defensive stance; by doing so, you can enhance your aptitude for emotional intelligence.

● Skill Development: Enhancing emotional intelligence is not an instantaneous process; nevertheless, it is an established fact that it can be refined through consistent practice.

Why Do Goals Fail To Produce Desired Outcomes For The Majority Of Individuals?

The reason for the failure of goal setting can be attributed to the fact that the individual responsible for setting the goals did not adhere to the necessary steps required to establish explicit and purposeful goals that provide a roadmap for achieving success. Here are the five reasons why most goals fail and how you can prevent these errors to establish formidable goals that guide you towards the wealth, success, happiness, and prosperity you desire.

1. Common objectives - numerous individuals establish highly generic objectives that fail to articulate a clear vision of what they intend to achieve. Objectives such as "acquiring a new residential property," "enhancing my financial gains," and "accumulating funds for leisure travel" fail to evoke motivation or provide a clearly defined aim for accomplishment.

In order to purchase a new residential property, it is advisable to establish a defined objective pertaining to the desired characteristics of the house such as its type, location, cost, appearance, size, and available amenities. Formulate a concise and precise vision of your desired outcome, and subsequently articulate your objective in writing. Establish your objectives and provide precise details. That is the crucial element in circumventing the pitfall of generic objectives.

Please provide as much detail and precision as you can. Formulate a distinct and coherent depiction of your intended target. Regardless of the objective, it is advised to articulate the goal with precision. If your objective is to augment the profitability of your enterprise, it is crucial to determine the precise magnitude of the desired increase in production.

Please select a specific monetary value or a percentage increase that you are committed to achieving. If you are in the process of organizing a vacation and aim to accumulate funds for this purpose, establish a specific budgetary allocation alongside selecting a destination and outlining planned activities.

Regardless of the objective, the greater the level of specificity employed, the higher the likelihood of its successful attainment. Why? As greater precision is applied in specifying one's desires, a corresponding enhancement occurs in the integration and fixation of those desires within the depths of one's subconscious.

Embedding your goals into your subconscious mind is a crucial element of achieving success. Once a clear vision of the goal has been established and internalized, one will discover that the actions taken tend to steer towards the achievement of said goal.

2. Insufficient capacity for measuring outcomes - in the event that the objective you establish lacks the means to evaluate your advancement, how

would you ascertain your proximity to achieving it? Establishing specific objectives will greatly facilitate the assessment of progress.

Generic objectives that are immeasurable are destined for failure. Assessing your progress enables you to make necessary adaptations throughout the journey to ensure you remain on course. By ensuring your objectives are quantifiable, they will gain enhanced efficacy.

3. Establishing unattainable objectives - if the objectives you establish are so extraordinary that they cannot be reasonably achieved within a defined timeframe, you will inevitably experience discouragement and eventually abandon them. Set ambitious objectives while ensuring they remain realistically attainable.

It is advantageous to set objectives that foster personal development, foster continuous learning, and push oneself beyond one's limits in order to attain them. Nonetheless, it would be ill-advised to jeopardize your prospects for success through the indulgence of unrealistic expectations. Solid objectives are characterized by their practicality and attainability.

4. Establishing goals that lack relevance - ensure that the goals you set align with your long-term plans and mission for your career and life. Frequently, individuals establish objectives that may appear appealing at the time or align with someone else's agenda, but do not align with your own plans.

Ensure that your objectives align with the desired outcome, otherwise, there may be no rationale for their pursuit. Do not squander your time pursuing objectives of little significance.

5. Failing to establish a timeline for attainment - an absence of time-bound objectives enables one to conveniently evade responsibility and forego taking action. Establishing a defined timeframe for achieving the objective instills a sense of responsibility to take decisive measures. It furthermore enables you to

modify your activities and implement corrections as needed.

If one establishes a goal of accumulating sufficient funds for a desired vacation in June, two years hence, diligent monitoring of progress and necessary adaptations can be undertaken. If a timeframe was not established and one waited until they were fully prepared, they might encounter the unforeseen financial consequences, resulting in the necessity to postpone the realization of their aspiration. That would be regrettable.

Continuing to Lead a Mindful Existence

When one continues to lead a conscientious existence, they are inevitably destined to embrace a physical reality abounding in profound joy and heartfelt contentment. Continuing to lead a purposeful existence entails thoroughly evaluating one's actions, decisions, and selections. You are making deliberate choices based on your virtues and personal authenticity.

What is conscious life?

A consciously lived existence entails a purposeful and extensively contemplated manner of living. It involves introspection followed by making informed decisions.

I am curious about the rationale behind your actions; delving into the intentions behind your decision-making processes. It is not aimlessly drifting in the current of existence, but rather executing a conscious and intentional maneuver.

Imagine visiting a retail establishment without having a preconceived notion of what you intend to procure. Engaging in conscientious living entails carefully considering a fundamental inventory of food items and discerning the meals you intend to assemble for dinner during the upcoming week. Practicing conscious living can be likened to proactively securing a flight ticket in advance, knowing the specific airline and destination to which you are headed, before reaching the airport.

Remarkably, the overwhelming majority do not reside in such a manner. They adhere to established norms, traditions imposed by their families, or conform to societal expectations.

What tangible results does one attain through intentional living?

Typically, we do not have the chance to live in a state of conscious awareness. From the moment of conception until our final breath, we are compelled to determine our course of action. Our parents instill within us a particular set of values, preferences, and career aspirations. Society reveals to us that success stems from residing in a specific locality, attaining a professional degree, procuring a particular type of residence, or owning a specific vehicle.

In addition to one's familial and societal sphere, international organizations are actively pursuing monetary gains by offering and promoting goods and services in order to satisfy the financial expectations of their stakeholders. By adopting a deliberate lifestyle, one can effectively confront and question every aspect of life. One could make an astute decision and choose to refrain from accepting anything that does not align with their values or beliefs.

What are my thoughts on the subject of awareness?

A potential strategy for discovering the solution is to reside in a state of anonymity. I resided in a state of ambiguity for a considerable duration of my existence, embracing the veracity of everything that was imparted to me by my family and society.

I selected a profession based on the remuneration.

I selected a relationship based on cultural norms and societal customs.

I selected a vocation based on its level of prestige.

I acquired a residence based on the discernment and guidance of the community.

Subsequently, each one of these components commenced to deteriorate, prompting my contemplation on the veracity of all the information I had been presented with. It is plausible that no individual possess an absolute understanding of what is in our best interests. What might have been effective for one person, one family, or even a particular generation may not be suitable for other individuals?

Body Image

I would visit the recreational area and observe my acquaintances engaging in a game of football. I abstained from participating as my disposition towards physical activity and football was unfavorable at the time. My preferred activity entailed returning to my residence to engage in play on my PlayStation console whilst consuming individual servings of confectionery. I did not enjoy optimal health during my childhood.

During a lunchtime encounter, my acquaintance made an observation, expressing that I possess a certain degree of corpulence, Jonathan.

This hurt me. This has caused me a significant amount of distress. This experience rendered me reticent and compelled me to refrain from engaging in conversation with others in order to avoid any potential disparaging remarks.

Upon entering secondary school, I experienced a slight reduction in my weight and adopted a more athletic lifestyle. Nevertheless, I did encounter the development of acne and dryness in my skin. The remarks made by individuals regarding the condition of my skin had a profoundly negative impact on my self-esteem, causing me to experience profound distress and reluctance in attending school.

Then there was Ken.

Ken, a pleasant individual in his early twenties, was gainfully employed and enjoyed the companionship of a small circle of acquaintances. However, Ken possessed a diminutive stature. As a result of this, he perceived himself to be less desirable than others and lacking appeal to women. Ken encountered significant challenges in developing a positive sense of self-worth. Consequently, the individuals who labeled him as 'short' were unaware of the profound emotional pain it caused him. It is highly likely that they did not take it into consideration.

While it is true that this particular area might not represent a major obstacle to my self-confidence. Despite having previous experiences of being overweight and having skin issues, I presently find myself in a relatively favorable state of health. Despite receiving compliments about my attractiveness from the opposite sex and being considered a good-looking individual, it took me a considerable amount of time to fully assimilate these observations. This was mainly due to my lingering self-perception, which had persisted from my days of being overweight and struggling with acne. The adverse experiences from previous years remained deeply ingrained within my subconscious, rendering them incredibly difficult to surmount.

Additionally, I faced the difficulty of attaining a well-defined abdominal six-pack over the course of several years. Fortunately, my current state of well-being outweighs any concern or preoccupation I may have once held. This pertains to the correlation between our observations of others and the subsequent impact on our self-perception and self-esteem, which can result in significant personal challenges when we are dissatisfied with our physical appearance relative to others.

Furthermore, I have encountered several aesthetically pleasing individuals who were regrettably incapable of perceiving their own allure. They were engaging in a process of self-evaluation and making comparisons with their peers. The issue of body image persists amid the challenges posed by conditions such as anorexia and bulimia. I extend my heartfelt affection and encouragement to those who are grappling with such challenges.

Regarding our physical beings, there exist dual facets:

1. Modifiable factors;

2. Things we can't.

In numerous instances, albeit not universally applicable, the aspects susceptible to modification often encompass our body weight and complexion. Certain individuals may exhibit dermatological conditions or medical conditions that impede their ability to achieve weight loss.

Elements beyond our control encompass facets like our inherent facial features, physical stature, and ocular characteristics.

Matters within our control can be subjected to inquiry regarding potential actions. As an illustration, I am currently undertaking measures to engage in physical exercise and maintain a nutritious diet in order to preserve my physical well-being. With regards to circumstances beyond our control, it is incumbent upon us to embrace them—an endeavor easier expressed than accomplished, as is the case with most aspects of life. Yet, negating or suppressing factors that lie outside our ability to alter will prove fruitless. Conversely, it is more advantageous to cultivate an appreciation for flaws.

Action:

Compose a comprehensive inventory highlighting both favorable and unfavorable aspects pertaining to your physical self.

On a daily basis, consistently remind yourself of the actions you undertake.

To separate the items you lack, categorize them into two groups. 1. How can I bring about a change in this situation? 2. What are the aspects that I cannot alter, yet I am prepared to embrace?

Employ the phrase 'I embrace and acknowledge myself unconditionally on a daily basis'. Initially, this task may prove challenging and give the impression of ineffectiveness, however, with time, it will gradually undergo reprogramming within the depths of the subconscious mind.

Do Not Entertain Unwarranted Negative Remarks.

Alternatively, if you are aware that you do not merit it. There exist individuals who consistently engage in detrimental discourse, persistently articulating unfavorable perspectives on their observations without regard for the impact it may have on others. There is no detriment in receiving criticism, provided that it is constructive in nature. By adopting this approach, it ultimately proves beneficial to the individual subjected to criticism.

Carefully consider the selection of your spoken language

"I will make an effort to accomplish the task" is distinct from "I will complete the task." "It is regrettable" carries a more profound impact; consider commencing with "Improvement could be achieved if..." "I possess exceptional capabilities" and "The potential exists," in addition to "It is feasible," and "There is a possibility of success." An additional guideline is to refrain from uttering words to others that you would find unpleasant if directed towards yourself.

Proactively Engage in Task Execution

Do not procrastinate in anticipating the initiative of others. Pursuing this course of action will likely yield the outcomes you seek; therefore, it is certain that you have no grounds for complaint.

Exercise mindfulness in the construction of your thoughts.

Exercise caution when engaging in negative thinking. However, there is no need to be too hard on yourself in such situations. Please be informed that the event occurred. Subsequently, remind yourself to adopt your current state of mind, specifically emphasizing the need to cultivate a more positive outlook.

Utilize Positive Imagery to Counteract Negative Thinking

Perceive your thoughts as distinct channels on your television screen. If you find yourself dissatisfied with the current channel, make a conscious decision to switch to a different one. An alternative approach entails perceiving negative thoughts as "irrelevant past occurrences". Recognize that these thoughts cannot destabilize you; you are situated above the proverbial bridge, unaffected by them. These visualizations are effective for certain individuals. If it does not yield the desired outcome, seek alternative visions that align with your goals.

Exercise impartiality and objectivity.

There are two factors contributing to your negative perception of others: either a lack of affinity towards the individual or their association with someone who evokes negative emotions in you. Regardless of the circumstances, experiencing distress is inevitable; therefore, endeavor to maintain a state of impartiality. However, if they have already acted unjustly towards you, then that is a different matter...

Most of the negativities lack solid foundation.

Exercise caution before accepting the immediate thoughts that cross your mind. Attempt to transform your thoughts into constructive notions. If you manage to achieve this, place your trust in those positive notions instead.

Two Words

Fly and fill. Detach yourself from pessimistic thinking. After capturing your attention, it is advisable to promptly distance yourself. Do not engage in conflict if the opposing force is too formidable. Just fly away. Leave it and go. Subsequently, infuse the vacant area with optimistic thoughts and concepts to guarantee its eradication upon its return. Make sure that it does not become ingrained within you. One cannot achieve spatial occupation unless something departs from that space. It is always beneficial to maintain positive thoughts in one's consciousness.

Utilize your heart as the guiding force in the majority of your decisions and actions.

The inherent characteristic of the mind is to display logic and exhibit a critical disposition. Illustrative of this point is the observation that when presented with a ratio of 9 commendable actions to 1 transgression, the human mind tends to fixate on the latter. Simultaneously, your heart will hold in high regard the benevolent actions bestowed upon you. Dwelling on past misdeeds can engender a pessimistic mindset. However, when employing one's emotions, an inclination towards identifying the shortcomings of others will not arise.

10

Unlocking Unwavering Self-Confidence: A Comprehensive 5-Step Guide

The cultivation of self-assurance entails an incessant undertaking that necessitates resolute determination and unwavering energy. Herein lies a set of guidelines to consider in the process of constructing your own:

Firstly, venture beyond the confines of your comfort zone.

To cultivate unwavering self-assurance, one must exhibit a readiness to venture beyond the confines of familiarity, thus enabling the pursuit of exceptional endeavors. You must awaken that intrinsic drive destined to surpass mediocrity.

It is possible that you possess a remarkably insightful notion which, if implemented, could greatly enhance the productivity and success of your organization. However, you may be at a loss as to how best to convey this idea to your superior. It is possible that you harbor affection for someone but have refrained from making any advances.

The issue arising from failing to act upon these desires is that you will effectively become stagnant in your current circumstances. Indeed, when one neglects to embark on new ventures, one inadvertently allows trepidation to deprive them of the radiance and vitality that life has to offer. You are further entrenching yourself within your established comfort zone. The deeply entrenched position you have occupied for an extended period.

Indeed, it can be a daunting endeavor to take the initial step into uncharted territory, whereby the possibility of encountering disappointment and subsequent embarrassment looms. However, upon deeper contemplation, one can ascertain that the underlying concept can be encapsulated in the term 'FEAR,' denoting the notion of False Evidence Appearing Real. What is the most detrimental outcome that could transpire in this situation? Frequently, you are simply engaging in excessive rumination. Venturing beyond your comfort zone may appear intimidating, yet it remains imperative in order to actualize your life's calling and attain unwavering self-assurance. This presents an opportunity for you to demonstrate your ability to accomplish anything you are determined to achieve.

Ultimately, what is the most catastrophic outcome that could potentially occur? You have the opportunity to collaborate with your boss and guide the company towards success, or the boss may decline the proposal. One may consider extending an invitation to that young lady or gentleman, thereby potentially receiving a response in the affirmative or negative. Consequently, one would obtain their answer efficiently, sparing valuable time otherwise spent speculating. In either scenario, it presents a mutually advantageous outcome.

The key to establishing unwavering self-assurance lies within oneself.

Certainly, I can assure you that in order to transcend the boundaries of your comfort zone, it is imperative to commence this endeavor by establishing incremental objectives, which, when assimilated, will culminate in the attainment of your overarching aspirations. Micro-goals are best understood as smaller components that make up the overarching objective at hand. When you divide your larger objectives into manageable portions, their achievement is greatly facilitated, and you will derive immense enjoyment during the process. Furthermore, this will help to cultivate your impetus, ensuring that you persistently strive towards the attainment of your desired objective.

Assuming that you possess a business idea or strategy that you aspire to communicate to your superior, although you have yet to summon the bravery to carry it out. An alternative approach is to decompose your primary objective into a series of sub-objectives that ultimately lead to comparable results. Commence your journey by taking incremental measures, regardless of their minuteness. Rather than embarking on a significant undertaking and becoming overwhelmed, commencing with smaller tasks will alleviate the pressure you may feel. By performing this action, you effectively facilitate comprehension and simplify subsequent actions.

Do you have a fondness for that particular individual, be it a girl or boy, yet find yourself lacking the fortitude to communicate your sentiments to them? However, it is possible that the individual in question is not currently in a relationship. Therefore, it is essential to initially establish a rapport with them, before delving into the intricacies of the matter at hand. Prior to extending an invitation for a date, acquaint yourself with their identity through the implementation of a brief conversation. Isn't that better? This does not appear to indicate that you are engaging in any form of stalking towards them.

Having expressed that point, it is important to acknowledge that establishing smaller objectives enables individuals to venture beyond their personal sphere of comfort. As you successfully attain your micro-objectives in succession, you will come to recognize that each and every minor accomplishment is instrumental in fostering the confidence necessary for propelling your progress. Encourage yourself to engage in daily extraordinary endeavors, and observe how this cultivates a profound sense of self-assurance.

What Is This?

However, let us begin by establishing my identity and the reasons for your consideration of my viewpoint.

Greetings, individuals. I am Alvaro Gutierrez and for the past eight years, I have been earning an income through online means, utilizing my laptop as a primary tool for my work. I am fortunate to have been graced with two delightful children, both of whom are twins, a daughter and a son, as well as a stunning wife whom I cherish deeply.

However, my journey commenced in the year 2000...

In the year 2000, I was gainfully employed at an automotive manufacturing facility located in the United Kingdom, committing myself to a rigorous work schedule that spanned seven consecutive days per week, a deliberate choice of my own volition. Despite the demanding nature of the work, life was splendid; I was receiving a satisfactory remuneration and fortuitously encountered the person who has since become my spouse. I was diligently occupied with my employment and focused on accumulating funds in order to purchase my property, an achievement I successfully accomplished one year subsequent to that.

During that period, I embarked on a supplemental venture involving the establishment of a Network Marketing enterprise. However, if I may speak frankly, I did not excel in this endeavor. It is possible that my Spanish accent contributed to my lack of success, although I present this notion with a touch of humor.

However, in the year 2007, it became apparent to me that my side hustle had consumed a significant amount of my financial resources and time, yet yielded minimal results. Subsequently, I chose to work in a corporate office for the subsequent five years, only to ultimately face termination. In retrospect, it appears that my shortcomings as an individual led to me displaying rudeness towards a customer, an unacceptable behavior that would no longer be tolerated. If you, Mrs. Green, happen to come across this, please accept my sincere apologies.

However, in summary, I found myself unemployed at that time, with the added responsibility of caring for my two-month-old infants, and without any source of income.

To succinctly summarize, I embarked upon drop-shipping on eBay and, in a condensed period of time, managed to accrue profits exceeding £900 (equivalent to approximately $1200). However, to achieve this, I found myself devoting rigorous 18-hour workdays, thereby severely limiting my interactions with my children. It is crucial to note that my intense motivation to secure sustenance for my family served as my driving force during this period.

Presently, I find myself incapable -- despite my extensive expertise -- of reproducing those outcomes... the market has become excessively oversaturated and eBay has imposed formidable barriers for newcomers seeking to enter the field. There is a considerable abundance of youngsters on Youtube expounding upon the lifestyle, yet regrettably, a majority of them possess an inadequate understanding, thereby merely imparting theoretical knowledge. So... while not entirely impossible, the task at hand is beset with significant challenges.

In the year 2015, Paypal detrimentally impacted my business by implementing a practice of withholding substantial sums of money that I earned through my diligent efforts. Their rationale rested on the notion that my level of sales had exceeded a certain threshold, thereby deeming me as a potential liability to their operations.

Suddenly, I found that approximately £5000 had been held in reserve for a duration of 6 months, if my recollection serves me correctly. This amount constituted the funds I had intended to allocate towards my living expenses and the settlement of eBay fees. In due course, I became incapacitated to remunerate the eBay fees, consequently resulting in the dissolution of my business due to my inability to continue conducting sales on their platform until the outstanding fees were settled.

The situation deteriorated to the extent that we found ourselves on the verge of homelessness, as our tenancy agreement expired and we faced financial constraints that prevented us from securing alternate accommodation. Compounding the issue was the fact that, since I primarily engaged in online sales, I lacked verifiable documentation of income to present to rental agencies. BIG MESS.

Ultimately, we found ourselves residing in my parents' exceedingly compact condominium, where we endured a year of slumber on the sofa. This arrangement required accommodating six individuals within a living space measuring approximately 50 square metres, a remarkably diminutive setting indeed. Transporting the children to school via public transportation, a journey that spans nearly an hour.Devoting four hours each day solely for commuting to and from school.Nightmare.

Subsequently, I reconstructed my business through the gracious assistance of a friend who kindly provided me with a loan of £3000, enabling me to settle my outstanding eBay fees and resume my entrepreneurial endeavors. Thank YOU. You are aware of your own identity.

I have acquired valuable insights through a challenging experience, enduring significant hardships not only on a financial level but also in terms of mental, physical, and spiritual aspects.

However, I ultimately regained control over my business. From that moment forward, I consistently employ the same strategies, which continue to yield profitable results. This applies not only to ecommerce but also to other social media tactics. Nonetheless, I have made adjustments to my overall approach.

Three: The Significance of Self-Assurance.

Self-assurance serves as the wellspring from which all other aspects of your life flow. You harness its power to attain and construct the various domains of your life. Consider this as the reservoir that powers your existence. It is evidently not the solid fuel; it is not something that can be reduced to a mere substance, yet it does indeed exist. It is important to note that individuals may often overlook the fact that possessing self-confidence empowers them to succeed in various facets of their existence.

Career

Self-assurance is crucial in the professional realm as, whether one favors it or not, organizations actively seek individuals with leadership qualities. When perusing the aforementioned job advertisement, wherein it states a preference for candidates at the entry-level, it can be inferred that individuals who proactively position themselves as prospective leaders are likely to progress within the organization. Regardless of whether you have applied for a job that appears to have limited prospects, once the business organization perceives you as having the potential to become a leader, they would be willing to make an investment in your development. They would have a significant stake in your personal growth and advancement. It is crucial to recognize that the success or failure of businesses hinges on their ability to proficiently develop ordinary employees into effective leaders.

Presently, the leadership role can assume diverse forms. You have the potential to assume the role of a frontline leader, which implies the opportunity to become a manager at a low-level position. You have the option to join the ranks of middle management, or alternatively, you have the potential for advancement to the position of vice-president or even chief executive officer. The outcome is contingent upon your actions.

It is crucial to comprehend that businesses are in great need of future leaders due to the fact that a significant majority of job applicants do so out of necessity to meet their financial obligations. They are simply seeking financial stability. They are not considering long-term perspectives; instead, they are primarily focused on their immediate requirements, and as a result, the majority of them fail to attain leadership positions. It lies completely beyond the framework of their role within the organization. They are merely seeking a resolution to the issue.

If an individual possesses a strong sense of self-assurance, they have the capacity to assume a leadership role. One can manifest the capability to accomplish tasks by harnessing the power of positive thinking. Not only can you serve as a source of inspiration through your productivity, but also by the emotional cues you emanate. You elicit a sense of optimism from those around you. You have the ability to enhance productivity in an organic manner due to your ability to motivate individuals.

These are the categories of individuals enterprises seek to cultivate and advance, as their ability to generate a sufficient number of leaders will enable them to outperform their rivals. Why? The competition between them is fueled by individuals who possess a notably transient mindset. Those individuals are simply seeking the opportunity to engage in labor and receive fair compensation for their efforts. Nothing more, nothing less. A company in which all staff members imbued with such a mindset will not achieve significant advancement. It will consistently be outperformed by organizations that possess capable leadership. Nevertheless, in order to attain a position of leadership, it is imperative that one possesses a sense of self-assurance.

Fifteen: Advancing in the Business World

There exist sectors where extroverted individuals are greatly sought after due to the importance placed on their communicative and sociable qualities, for instance, within networking companies and brokerage firms. Nevertheless, as the digital era continues to advance, the attributes of introverted individuals are increasingly gaining prominence in the market.

In contrast to the previous era characterized by one-way communication and limited interaction, the advent of the digital platform has facilitated active engagement among individuals through content sharing. This necessitates careful consideration and an inclusive approach that encourages individuals to engage. Given the inherent qualities possessed by introverts, they are destined for success as future marketers.

1. Meaningful Content.

Numerous enterprises are transitioning from conventional in-person sales to digital marketing strategies. In addition to significant cost savings, they are able to extend their reach to a broader demographic. Nevertheless, this phenomenon results in internet congestion.

Numerous advertisements employ flashing, popping, sparkling, and various forms of exhibition to captivate your attention. These captivate the interest of individuals in a manner akin to that of extroverted personalities. However, they can be effortlessly disregarded, particularly when interacting online as people have the option to exhibit apathy and pass judgment. The key determinant of a successful marketing campaign in the digital realm is the quality of its content.

Introverts possess a distinct advantage in this domain. They engage in actively listening, keen observation, and cognitive processing of information, which empowers them to generate profoundly perceptive and contemplative content that possesses the capacity to captivate individuals of all backgrounds. Subsequently, individuals are urged to partake in the initiative by means of sharing, endorsing, retweeting, and similar actions.

2. Direct and succinct communication.

In the realm of commerce, the essence lies in the transfer of communication. This consistently marks the initial stage in cultivating intrigue within prospective clients. Nevertheless, as the internet becomes increasingly saturated, the focus of audiences has constricted to mere fractions of a second. Extroverted individuals frequently engage in initiating conversations through casual exchanges, employing a similar approach within the realm of online marketing. Nonetheless, the majority of individuals tend to abstain from such activities if possible, and once more, while ensconced in the comfort of their residences, they are able to do so. This concept resonates strongly with individuals who possess introverted tendencies. They have a aversion to engaging in casual conversations, thus opting to be direct and concise. Communications that promptly convey their intended information tend to receive a higher level of focused attention.

3. Stronger Relationships.

If extroverts are primarily concerned with pursuing "dates", their opposing counterparts are inclined to establish "long-term commitments" in the realm of digital platforms. This indicates that they possess a higher level of willingness to actively engage and respond to different viewpoints expressed by readers following content sharing, whereas their counterparts typically content themselves with receiving simple likes. In today's contemporary society, connectivity assumes a paramount significance, surpassing the importance of extensive coverage. In this regard, introverts serve as the key individuals when striving to foster interpersonal connections, both offline and on digital platforms.

4. Initiates and Values Collaboration.

It is frequently observed on the internet that there is a prevalence of content that emanates individualistic sentiments. There exist certain marketing campaigns that excessively draw attention to themselves, unaware that they alienate a greater number of individuals rather than captivate them. Contrarily, introverts uphold the principle of cooperative endeavors. They acknowledge that the collective collaboration of intellectuals and various stakeholders can generate impactful communications and more significant outcomes.

5. Disposition towards Content Sharing from External Sources.

A robust digital environment is built on the principles of reciprocity. Marketers have the opportunity to enhance their reach and establish a stronger level of trustworthiness by disseminating meaningful content shared by others, while ensuring complete citation of the original source and copyright ownership. When comparing these two personality types, it can be observed that introverts exhibit a greater willingness towards embracing this concept, and they may take the initiative to engage in such behavior.

6. Authenticity and Transparency.

Identifying falsehoods online is a straightforward task and serves as the clandestine factor in fostering skepticism among internet users. Contrarily, introverts exhibit a remarkable degree of transparency in their communication, consistently avoiding any embellishment or ostentation in their choice of words. In more concise language, the phenomenon can be described as a direct correlation between appearance and reality. They do not conceal anything beneath the rock, and they lack any justification to do so.

In certain instances, conducting business may not necessarily entail direct personal interaction. With the emergence of technological advancements, individuals of introverted nature have the opportunity to reside in the tranquility of their own residences, yet adeptly execute their professional duties on par with their extroverted peers. As frequently emphasized by numerous accomplished individuals, make use of your strengths and effectively leverage them towards achieving your goals. One is not obligated to conform to the actions of others at all times. Introverted individuals possess a cunning ability to veer from conventional paths and forge their own trajectories through unorthodox means. All that is required is for you to adequately arm yourself with knowledge, and as you peruse this book, you have already achieved that.

There exists no distinct constituent that enables the acquisition of power, as it is already an intrinsic attribute within oneself. Your exceptionally introspective intellect simply requires recognition of its capacities, as well as the requisite self-assurance, to unlock its utmost potential.

2.3 Intelligence

Intelligence plays a significant role in shaping our emotions, actions, and cognitive processes. The manifestation of intelligence is primarily gauged through IQ assessments, notwithstanding the recognition of the limited accuracy or limited utility associated with official IQ examinations. Their errors stem from the contextually specific nature of different cultures and the challenges encountered in capturing and measuring the experiences of individuals. Intelligence can be defined as the capacity to acquire and possess knowledge as well as demonstrate aptitude for acquiring and honing various skills. This indicates that the brain possesses the capacity to acquire knowledge and retain it consistently.

Emotional intelligence pertains to the realm of emotions and is synonymous with emotional intellect. The phenomenon of emotional experience is universally encountered by individuals of the human species, serving as a profound means of establishing shared connections among those who engage in it. It is a universally acknowledged fact that human beings possess the capacity to experience emotions, engage in cognitive processes, and undergo distinct life experiences. Emotional Intelligence, also known as EI, encompasses the capacity to perceptively perceive and comprehend the emotional state of others, thus equipping individuals with the skills to effectively discern and navigate interpersonal dynamics, foster harmonious relationships, and assertively advocate for one's own needs and boundaries. Emotional Intelligence (EI) refers to an individual's capacity to effectively attain knowledge and competencies pertaining to the realm of emotions. Upon careful consideration, it becomes evident that this concept possesses an extensive range of practical applications. It could encompass the capacity of an individual to provide solace to another during moments of turmoil, or it might pertain to an individual's capability to terminate a relationship when it is deemed justified.

Exhibiting emotional intelligence necessitates a significant capacity for empathy. The development of emotional intelligence is imperative because genuine emotional intelligence involves the ability to discern when to demonstrate empathy and actively engage in attentive listening.

Have you ever encountered the phenomenon of establishing a deep connection with another individual purely through the act of attentive listening? It is an impactful encounter that eludes the grasp of many individuals, even if they subjectively believe to have experienced it previously. Certain individuals have yet to encounter the profound understanding that can stem solely from attentive listening. This phenomenon is attributable to our inclination to engage in simultaneous speaking, contentious exchanges, and various linguistic tactics aimed at asserting our dominance.

When an individual is attentive and demonstrates active listening, it is evident that they possess a genuine capacity for empathy. Let us further explore the concept of empathy. Empathy entails experiencing and understanding the emotional distress of another individual. One can empathize with their experience by either drawing upon personal encounters or perceiving it as analogous to alternative patterns of behavior. Empathy is the emotional experience that arises when witnessing someone contending with a task or burden that is arduous for them to attain or bear. It involves a deep sense of understanding and resonance, stemming from personal knowledge of the difficulties associated with carrying or attempting to transport exceptionally sizable objects. Therefore, you cease your current tasks and proceed towards their location in order to extend assistance. This can be attributed to your demonstration of understanding and compassion towards their hardship. Your willingness to assist stemmed from your empathy towards the individual, and your decision to offer aid was guided by your recognition of the support you would have desired had you found yourself in a comparable circumstance.

There are certain extremes associated with this scenario. For instance, when individuals are confronted with a dire circumstance entailing a choice between life and death, their innate survival instinct compels them to prioritize self-preservation above all other considerations. They will endeavor to extricate themselves from an engulfed structure, such as a burning edifice, even before attending to the rescue of a dear companion. Please bear in mind that we are discussing the utmost extreme scenario in this context. This represents a unique instance where empathy tends to prevail. In instances such as these, the human psyche demonstrates great volatility and the potential to exhibit primal behavior in response to fear or a loss of control.

Undertake an analysis of the instances in which you habitually appraise individuals based on their behavior.

Perhaps there was an individual who was operating a vehicle at an excessively low speed on the thoroughfare with which you have become accustomed. You become exasperated by the individual's conduct, and quietly pass judgment within your thoughts, strongly criticizing them and using offensive epithets in your mind. There may be additional variables involved; it is possible that the individual is experiencing a malfunction with their engine, prompting them to cautiously drive to the automobile repair facility. Had you been aware of that information, would you have exhibited such a prominent emotional response? If that is not the case, I would suggest contemplating the factors that could foster a similar level of enthusiasm and disposition towards the driver, prior to acquiring this knowledge. This task is highly complex to cultivate and necessitates personal growth. As you endeavor to cultivate empathy, make an effort to extend your empathy toward individuals whom you may perceive as bothersome or aggravating. These cases represent considerable challenges, yet they provide an invaluable opportunity for you to cultivate and enhance your abilities to empathize with others, a skill that will prove invaluable in situations requiring empathy. You will have enhanced the strength of this muscle.

Life experience typically facilitates the cultivation of empathy. Frequently, individuals who are initially self-centered require a humbling experience or a consequential event in order to cultivate a heightened sense of empathy. Chances are, you have come across one of these individuals. They appear to possess an amiable demeanor, however, upon further acquaintance, it becomes evident that their presence proves displeasing to you. It has come to your attention that there is a lack of opportunity to fully enjoy oneself, as well as an evident preoccupation with self-centered thoughts. This individual has not encountered a circumstance where their sense of self-importance is humbled and they are reminded of their connection to other individuals. This individual has yet to experience the profound impact that can leave one feeling utterly shattered and completely disintegrated.

Why? Due to the provision of protection and facilitation bestowed upon this individual. There exists a distinct category of individuals who are raised with such extensive privileges that they fail to assimilate within the wider populace. They are social climbers. This phenomenon is frequently observed among individuals belonging to the millennial generation. The individual identified as a social climber perceives interpersonal connections not merely as a means of emotional support, but rather as a pathway to ascend the socioeconomic hierarchy. Do not hesitate to hold these individuals accountable. Within the realm of social media, to illustrate, the longing for approval in the form of likes and followers is in fact a manifestation of their inherent void in self-confidence. If you happen to encounter an individual of such nature, endeavor to engage in a tactful conversation with said person. It can be effortless to become engrossed in the realm of online existence. Encourage individuals to occasionally set aside their mobile devices. In order to establish a clear preference for face-to-face interaction unencumbered by the use of electronic devices, it is advisable to communicate your intention and assert your requirement to the individuals concerned.

Growth

Apprehension may impede your ability to embark on personal development in your life. For individuals, progress holds significance in fostering personal development and stimulating a sense of fulfillment in our existence. As we traverse the journey of life, it is inherent for us to undergo growth and transformation with the passage of time. However, the pervasive grip of fear has the potential to impede this natural progression. Consider the prospect of attending a fitness center and engaging in strength training exercises. As you engage in prolonged physical exertion, your musculature will fortify, owing to the adaptive response of your muscles to increased resistance. Subsequently, you will progressively augment the weights you are lifting as your muscular strength progressively advances. The functioning of our minds closely resembles that of our muscles. By subjecting ourselves to novel situations or experiences and pushing our limits, our cognitive faculties can undergo expansion, so to speak. During this process, we can continually expose ourselves to novel circumstances, thereby enlarging both our comfort zone and our cognitive capacities. The objects and concepts that we perceive as novel and intimidating will undergo a transformation, leading us to expand our definition of what we consider secure and reassuring. This process entails the incorporation of an increasing number of elements into our sphere of safety and comfort, several of which would have been viewed as unaccustomed and alarming in earlier times.

Apprehension Encourages a Disposition Towards Negativity or Pessimism

In the presence of fear, our attention fixates on potential hazards rather than the possible benefits that may arise from the triggering circumstances. Consequently, fear engenders pessimism rather than optimism. Negativity impedes our progress as it steers our focus away from the potential benefits of a situation, and instead fixates on the potential drawbacks. May I inquire about potential risks or hazards that I should be aware of? "What potential drawbacks could arise from this situation?" When endeavoring to enhance self-esteem, maintaining an optimistic outlook is crucial. Elevated self-esteem is founded upon positivity, whereas diminished self-esteem is rooted in negativity. When striving to enhance one's self-esteem, it is imperative to prioritize positive aspects and cultivate a sense of optimism; unfortunately, succumbing to fear impedes our ability to engage in these constructive practices.

Fear impedes our cognitive function.

This section will introduce the source of our concerns, commonly known as "the stimulus." The stimulus encompasses a wide range of triggering factors, including encounters with aggressive animals, invitations to social events, or unexpected encounters with former acquaintances seeking conversation. This term serves as a comprehensive descriptor for the underlying cause of our discomfort.

The sensation of fear impedes the cognitive processing in our brains, as the fight or flight mechanism, inherent in our neurophysiology, operates at a faster pace than our cognitive faculties can accommodate. During the era of ancestral humans, were we to allocate time towards the proper handling and deliberation of the bear that stood before us, it is highly probable that the creature would have already consumed us before we could reach a consensus. This is the reason why fear hinders the cognitive processing of the stimulus. In the present era, however, this can prove to be more detrimental than beneficial. The presence of fear hinders the ability to deliberately and consciously analyze the stimulus, which encompasses rational thinking grounded in factual information and careful consideration of the advantages and disadvantages.

Should we choose to permit such an occurrence, we might ascertain that the stimulus presents no imminent danger and that, despite feeling apprehensive, we shall proceed regardless. Frequently, this is likely to be true, however, before making a determination, it is imperative that we first analyze the stimulus. The challenge lies in the fact that once gripped by fear, it becomes exceedingly difficult to extricate oneself from this state and commence a rational analysis of the situation. We will explore several approaches to accomplish this later within the confines of this chapter.

Fear does not allow for compromise.

A remarkable aspect of the human species lies in our capacity to engage in compromise. If we judge something to be excessive or insufficient, we can arrive at a mutually agreeable compromise, without categorically rejecting it. When one experiences a fear response, it manifests as an unequivocal binary reaction, allowing for no room for negotiation or compromise due to the intense and agitated state induced by fear. If one were to rationally contemplate the potential overwhelming nature of a particular circumstance, it is conceivable that they may opt to instead adopt a more balanced approach or pursue an alternative course of action. Take, for instance, the scenario mentioned earlier. Suppose you receive an invitation to accompany unfamiliar individuals in an unfamiliar locality to a bar outing. In such a situation, you may undergo an initial sensation of fear upon being asked, which is then succeeded by the inclination to provide a definitive acceptance or refusal. If, however, you were able to transcend the influence of fear, it is plausible that you could have arrived at the determination that you are amenable to socializing with these unfamiliar individuals. Nevertheless, the prospect of venturing into a new neighborhood with them may have appeared overwhelming to you given the circumstances. Therefore, you could have expressed your inclination to only partake in a single drink in a nearby location before returning to the familiarity of your own dwelling, allowing them to proceed to the aforementioned new neighborhood, or alternatively, proposed a compromise of similar nature.

Fundamental Tenets Of Objective Establishment

These 20 fundamental principles will rejuvenate your life, instilling in you a fresh sense of vitality, enthusiasm, and fervor. They will propel you forward, bridging the gap between your current position and your desired destination, with unprecedented speed that exceeds even your most audacious aspirations.

1 - Intense Passion

The primary principle of goal setting is to possess an intense and unwavering aspiration. This is not a skill that can be acquired through training; it is either innate or non-existent. You may possess the ability to maintain concentration on your task or objective for a brief duration; however, in the absence of an intense aspiration, it is inevitable that you will subsequently diminish your momentum.

2 - Establish a Singular Primary Objective

Approximately 95% of the American population currently lacks identifiable objectives or aspirations. Among the remaining 5% of Americans who possess goals, the majority tend to establish an excess of objectives. Why does this present an issue? Because without a major definite purpose or goal, one lacks clarity and is no closer to accomplishing any of their goals than the 95% of Americans who do not set goals at all. It is imperative that your goals are articulate and precise.

3 - Establish objectives that are attainable while still challenging you.

On numerous occasions, we tend to engage in one of two actions when establishing objectives: either we establish our goals excessively ambitious or excessively modest; seldom do we succeed in setting them at an optimal level. This aspect of goal setting can prove to be exceedingly challenging, particularly in the absence of extensive experience with this method.

By establishing insubstantial targets, we consistently fall short of realizing our utmost capabilities and fail to lead a life of self-actualization. By establishing excessively ambitious objectives, we expose ourselves to the possibility of becoming disheartened due to the significant distance between the goal and our current position.

4 - Establish Goals that are Quantifiable

Objectives should be quantifiable primarily for the purpose of being able to monitor your progress. It is comparable to monitoring your progress during your commute to work by operating your vehicle. When commuting to work by car, you are aware of both the distance covered and the remaining distance to be traveled.

It is insufficient to merely state, 'I desire to attain physical fitness.' How can one determine whether they have achieved physical fitness? Rather, I would recommend providing additional details. For instance, you could state, 'I am able to complete a mile in 7 minutes'. It is evident, accurate, and capable of being quantified.

5 - Document Your Objectives

Ensure that when documenting your objective, it is unambiguous, affirmative, and expressed in the present tense. One illustration of this can be seen in the statement, "My annual income amounts to $100,000." By merely documenting your objective, you are bringing it to life; you are transforming your goal into a tangible manifestation.

6 - Establish a Target Date for Accomplishment

According to Parkinson's Law, work will naturally expand to fill the allotted time for its completion. Consequently, the more time we allocate ourselves to complete a task or achieve a goal, the longer it will take us to accomplish it. Henceforth, it is imperative that we acquire the skill of effectively employing Parkinson's Law to our benefit by establishing condensed timeframes within which we can accomplish our objectives or tasks.

7 - Identify and Assess all Potential Obstacles and Setbacks

Encountering obstacles should not discourage you, but rather assist you in avoiding any unforeseen setbacks that may arise, thus enabling you to formulate the most efficacious strategies possible. By acknowledging impediments, your mind should subsequently commence contemplating potential resolutions to address these envisaged circumstances.

8 - Develop Your Key Indicators

An illustration of a primary indicator would be the quantity of cold calls that you will initiate. Following the determination of the primary indicator, you proceed to establish a target for that particular metric.

This particular measure is designed to assist you in discerning the utmost critical tasks that necessitate daily completion, thereby advancing your progression towards achieving the desired objective. By prioritizing and fully committing to accomplishing the task at hand, you can effectively reduce the time spent on this task by 80% compared to attempting to complete it through smaller increments.

Joy and self-acknowledgment operate in cohesion.

According to Robert Holden, as stated in his book Happiness Now!, there is a symbiotic relationship between joy and self-acknowledgment. Truly, the extent to which one recognizes oneself is directly correlated to the level of happiness one experiences. Increasing your level of self-acknowledgment will enhance your capacity to recognize, obtain, and derive pleasure from accomplishments and experiences. Therefore, you derive equal pleasure from what you embrace, as you are deserving of it.

Primarily, the cultivation of self-awareness demands that we foster self-compassion. We will only be able to strengthen our self-relationship, which has so far eluded us, when we can fully grasp and absolve ourselves from the obligations that we previously believed were our own.

In order to adopt a more affectionate stance that is advantageous to our own well-being - a fundamental indicator of self-acceptance - it is imperative to recognize that hitherto, we have primarily felt compelled to demonstrate our worth to others, much like the way we initially believed we had to conform to the critical authority of our parents. Our endorsement seeking practices henceforth (whether misguided or not) has reflected the legacy of our ancestors' exclusive affection.

An empirical inquiry, similar to an authentic examination of what I would categorize as our nearly pervasive situation, undeniably engenders heightened self-compassion. It is inherently compassionate that we can ascertain means of nurturing greater self-love and perceiving ourselves with admiration and respect due to our resolute willingness to confront (and strive against) what we have diligently cultivated and come to acknowledge regarding our own being.

It could be posited that each of us bears remnants of "scars resulting from the experience of conditional love" from a distant past. We find ourselves among those who are experiencing temporary physical limitations. Moreover, recognizing and embracing our shared humanity can foster a sense of compassion and goodwill that extends beyond our own selves, encompassing others as well.

In order to cultivate greater self-acceptance, it is crucial that we consistently remind ourselves (with increasing conviction, if possible) that considering our predominantly biased and narrow-minded perspectives, we have made earnest efforts in our actions. In light of the circumstances, it is imperative that we reevaluate any lingering notions of assigning fault, as well as our multitude of internal responses and derogatory comments. We ought to confront and explore those aspects of ourselves that we tend to ignore, and, as active agents in our own healing process, approach self-rejection or denial with empathy and understanding. Therefore, we may now proceed with dismantling inaccurately portrayed sentiments of culpability and shame, based on assessments that inadequately represented our reasonable capabilities at the given moment.

The renowned French saying, "Tout comprendre, c'est tout excuser" (literally, "To understand all is to excuse all"), constitutes a principle that ought to be applied in various situations, both towards ourselves and towards others. By undertaking such an analysis, we can gain a comprehensive understanding of the underlying reasons that limited our actions in the past with a specific objective in focus. Subsequently, we will undoubtedly find it conceivable to grant ourselves forgiveness for this behavior, and furthermore, refrain from engaging in its repetition in the future.

In order to develop greater self-acceptance, it is imperative that we recognize and appreciate the fact that we are not solely responsible for any one aspect of our lives, be it our communication, understanding, or any other less defined behaviors. Our actions have been limited by a combination of fundamental principles and scientific concepts. Moving forward, it is undeniable that we can - and typically should - take responsibility for the consequences of our actions that have caused harm or mistreated others. Regardless, if we are to effectively cultivate self-tolerance, it is imperative that we approach this endeavor with an abundance of empathy and forgiveness embedded within our beings. We must grasp a specific concept, taking into account our inherent programming up until that moment; our ability to behave differently was severely limited.

Do Something That Brings You Joy.

I was frustrated. I had an extensive list of tasks to address on that particular day, including a substantial amount of administrative work related to the waste management program for which I was responsible for overseeing multiple projects. I experienced a profound sense of dissatisfaction with my own identity and found significant discontentment in my occupation, to the extent that on certain occasions, it compelled me to seclude myself and shed tears.

That day, the occurrence of lunchtime provided a modest alleviation amidst the unpleasant circumstances. On account of the favorable weather conditions, I ventured to the park on that particular summer day. Curiously, it appears that

England once possessed such recreational spaces, albeit at the time of composing this rendition, our excursions are presently limited to a single daily outing to ensure social distancing amidst the prevailing coronavirus outbreak.

On that particular occasion, I refrained from descending the slide or initiating the act of feeding the ducks with bread crumbs (apologies for the unconventional phrasing, but I considered retaining it for amusement purposes).

I am admittedly taking a circuitous route in recounting this narrative. Nonetheless, I proceeded to retrieve my notepad and commence devising the intricate plot for my upcoming work of fantasy literature. Edge of Perfection. I became fully immersed in the process of conceptualizing the narrative, causing my worries to evade my consciousness and allowing the resumption of joy within me. Upon the conclusion of the lunch, I experienced a melancholic sentiment as I prepared to depart. However, the remarkable sensation that surged within me was unparalleled in its intensity.

I experienced a sense of purpose, joy, and exhilaration.

When we engage in activities that do not align with our genuine passions, we fail to effectively convey our true selves. Hence, it is apparent to me that individuals may experience significant unhappiness within their employment. I have experienced dissatisfaction in previous employment endeavors due to a lack of personal affinity and an absence of engagement in activities aligned with my passions.

I am currently in a favorable position where I possess a clear understanding of my life goals and aspirations. It simply boils down to persistently striving for it and enhancing my expertise in marketing and sales. My aspiration is to become a professional author and public speaker. In addition, I provide coaching and mentoring services to individuals. I love it.

These experiences fill me with exhilaration and offer me the gratifying sensation of embracing my true self.

Speaking is the activity that profoundly alters my entire world. Currently, I am experiencing a tingling sensation, however, while delivering a speech, there is truly no sensation that can compare. When I am sharing my insights on subjects that I believe can benefit others, I experience a sense of invincibility. At present, I must admit that I do not possess the highest level of proficiency in public speaking. However,

I possess a fervent passion for it and consistently strive to enhance my skills.

I would like for you to discover your passion or purpose. It may not necessarily involve verbal communication, yet there exists some form of interaction. Possible alternative: Some potential activities to consider could include dancing, creative writing, fine arts such as painting, physical activities like running or playing tennis, engaging in video game design, honing baking skills, or exploring the art of ballroom dancing. One should never feel embarrassed about the true nature of the matter. Furthermore, the individuals who will criticize you are solely those who are hesitant to pursue their aspirations or venture outside of their familiar surroundings.

It is possible that you are already aware of its definition, or you may still be unfamiliar with it.

If you choose to engage in this activity, ensure that you allocate time for it on a daily basis, as doing so will enable your authentic self to emerge and consequently enhance your self-esteem.

If you do not wish to do so, that is perfectly acceptable. Please do not feel burdened as you may not be aware, but it is important to dedicate sufficient time towards discovering your true calling. Reflecting upon the activities that brought you joy during your childhood consistently proves beneficial.

I am currently composing this piece with minimal exertion, and I derive immense satisfaction from the process. I enthusiastically endorse the book 'Super Attractor' authored by Gabby Bernstein, as it serves as an exceptional resource for cultivating positivity and wellness. This analysis explores the significance of prioritizing emotional well-being over the end result. When we experience a sense of contentment, everything tends to harmonize more seamlessly. Think about it? Do you derive pleasure from engaging in activities that align with your personal interests and passions?

Consequently, what is the outcome if the desired results are not attained when one engages in proactive measures? One would reacquaint themselves with the joy of engaging in their passion and living in the present moment, seek counsel and support from an experienced advisor or teacher, and then resume their pursuit.

Action:

If you possess a clear understanding of your genuine passion, allocate a minimum of twenty minutes per day (or preferably, more if feasible) within your schedule to cultivate and engage in your beloved pursuit.

If you are unsure, then allocate a sufficient amount of time to determine your true passion. I will provide a set of inquiries below to assist with the matter at hand.

Inquiries to initiate your pursuit of your passions:

May I inquire about the activities that brought you joy during your childhood?

● In the event that you only had a remaining timeframe of six months, what course of action would you choose? (I apologize for any perceived overemphasis on the tragic aspect, but it provided me with assistance.)

● What skills or activities do you excel at or derive pleasure from? (You are also permitted to derive enjoyment from activities at which you lack proficiency!)

● What causes you to disregard all other matters when engaged in that particular task? (I kindly request that you refrain from suggesting inebriation or substance abuse as a response to this question.)

May I inquire as to the particular skill or ability that you would choose to cultivate, if granted the opportunity?

The implications of pessimistic thoughts and their correlation with clinical depression

Indeed, this particular aspect leads us back to the relationship between pessimistic thoughts and the state of depression, as it has been observed that individuals experiencing depression are inclined towards negative thinking patterns. The negativity arises solely from the current functioning of your brain. You are facing difficulties in assimilating the hormones responsible for inducing happiness, thus preventing your body from reaping the advantages in your conduct. If one experiences no sense of joy in their current actions, they may not perceive any rationale to endeavor towards modification. You perceive matters as devoid of purpose, and this perception hampers your ability to summon the motivation required for initiating change. Once more, we are confronted with the recurrence of this cycle - the propagation of negativity begets more negativity.

Consistently, there is a prevailing sense that your depression is being validated, and in some cases, exacerbating, due to your incapacity to genuinely alter your state of mind. One is unable to overcome the negative thoughts due to their self-defeating and self-perpetuating nature.

Despite harboring a dislike for these thoughts, one believes they are warranted, leading to inward resentment and self-loathing. You start ascribing the identity of a failure to yourself or convince yourself that you possess inherent flaws, lack value, and are unworthy of esteem, achievement, or happiness. These thoughts impede your progress, exacerbate your depression, and render it increasingly difficult to break free from the cycle.

Nevertheless, it is within your power to bring about a transformation in your outlook, thereby diminishing negative thoughts and mitigating certain manifestations of depression. Although it may not be possible for you to instantly alter your brain chemistry to experience immediate pleasure, you will, however, be able to recognize and appreciate the significance of utilizing positive speech and conduct. You will witness the transformative power of positivity in shaping the outcome.

The Impact of Pessimistic Thoughts on Your Life

Are you of the opinion that the future will be superior to the present? Can you definitively assert that you hold the conviction that tomorrow will exceed yesterday? This question can be responded to succinctly using a simple affirmation, negation, or possibility. It is interesting to contemplate that your response could potentially influence the events of your future. Our lives are shaped by the thoughts that we hold.

I would like to pose a query: What prompts us to excessively concern ourselves with various matters? What is the reason behind our inclination to anticipate the most unfavorable outcome in every circumstance? It is due to our sincere concern. The factor that prompted your purchase of this book revolves around the concept of moving closer to eliminating negative thinking from your life. Now, let us try.

Negativity arises as a result of cognitive processes. Frequently, this thought process is initiated by negative previous encounters. These previous encounters may manifest as instances of disappointment, denial, underestimation, prejudice, and the like. Should an individual encounter recurrent failures throughout their life, there emerges a gradual cultivation of a novel cognitive framework. They could adopt a belief in the implausibility of aspirations materializing. They may also soon come to the realization that achieving success in life is unattainable. They will develop a pessimistic viewpoint and apply it universally in all circumstances. They experience numerous instances throughout the course of their lives. In summary, they adopt a pessimistic outlook.

A pessimistic individual is one whose cognitive processes are primarily focused on negative thoughts, which in turn influence their emotions and subsequently manifest as negative behavioral reactions, leading to the expression of a pessimistic attitude. The perpetuity of this cycle engulfs their entire essence. They tend to adopt a pessimistic outlook on life as a result of their innate tendencies.

Individuals with a pessimistic mindset, or those who tend to engage in negative thinking, exhibit consistent patterns in their behavior and thought processes. This pattern derives from a persistent recurrence of pessimistic thoughts. These patterns encompass four primary categories of negative thinking. The inclination towards an "all-or-nothing" mindset arises from a desire for perfection. The attainment of perfection is imperative; anything falling short thereof is inherently deemed a failure. An alternative perspective involves discounting any positive aspects. It swiftly refutes any optimism and promptly reaches the inference that every aspect of existence will solely yield disillusionment. Additionally, negative self-labeling entails the acceptance and acknowledgement of one's own shortcomings. This line of thinking presupposes a lack of worthiness to receive love and appreciation. Catastrophizing represents the final category among significant forms of negative thought patterns. It magnifies and highlights the most negative aspects of any given situation, exaggerating their significance.

Residing within a constrained system of beliefs inhibits our progress towards the desired life we aspire to possess. You are delving deeper into a predicament from which you had previously desired to escape. Have you been persistently immersed in a pattern characterized by pessimism and negativity? Would you be willing to acknowledge that it has had a profound impact on your life?

Consider the transformative impact that adopting a positive mindset can have on the trajectory of your life. It is a formidable enigma that has been transmitted across successive lineages. We simply need to acquire the knowledge of integrating it into our everyday routines.

Modulating Emotional Responses in Response to Surroundings

The ambiance surrounding you carries significant influence over your emotional state, especially if you possess a strong capacity for empathy. You harness the surrounding atmosphere, assimilating its influence—when the atmosphere is fraught with tension and unease, it is inevitable that you will internalize that apprehension too. If one perceives the environment as hazardous, they will experience fear. You are likely to experience distress in a situation where you are surrounded by individuals who are also experiencing sadness.

Hence, it is of utmost importance to exercise caution when selecting the company you associate with. In order to maintain a joyful disposition, it is imperative to surround oneself with affable individuals who exhibit kindness and respect towards you. If you aspire to attain a sense of tranquility and serenity, accompanied by a deep and unwavering self-assurance within your immediate surroundings, it is imperative that you find yourself immersed in an environment that cultivates precisely such an atmosphere of calmness and relaxation. Your body's behavior will be influenced by the behavior of others. You shall experience a sense of tranquility once you perceive through the body language of others that there exists no imminent cause for alarm. You are likely to experience a boost of energy when those in your immediate vicinity exhibit signs of vigor.

In essence, as human beings, our inherent nature is that of social creatures. We derive our means of communication from our surroundings. The emotions of our friends and family resonate within the atmosphere, permeating our surroundings and wielding a significant influence over our being.

To alter your emotional state, it is advisable to refrain from dwelling upon your surrounding circumstances. Is it strict? Does it possess a harsh and discomfiting quality? Do you experience feelings of affection or security? If you are unable to affirm that you experience happiness and contentment within your relationship, it is advisable to contemplate disengaging from the detrimental atmosphere.

Environments characterized by toxicity have a tendency to foster further instances of such behavior. Adverse surroundings foster pessimism. It is permissible to eliminate those negative and toxic elements from your life, regardless of their familiarity or comfort. Your psychological well-being will greatly benefit from this action.

Additionally, should you desire to create a positive and invigorating atmosphere, it would be advisable to immerse yourself in an environment characterized by positive energy. Associate yourself with reliable companions. Please select lively music that inspires you to engage in physical activity. One is significantly more inclined to derive pleasure if the prevailing conditions in one's surroundings are conducive to such enjoyment.

Ultimately, it will be necessary for you to acknowledge that there is a correlation between your emotions and the surrounding environment. One's emotional state often mirrors the surrounding environment, and this is perfectly acceptable. Nevertheless, if you happen to find yourself in a detrimental environment, it becomes necessary for your own well-being and the well-being of those close to you to rectify the situation. One need not tolerate toxic individuals, regardless of their familial ties You are fully entitled to terminate any relationship, be it familial, romantic, or platonic, if you perceive it as a detrimental environment that necessitates disengagement.

Please be reminded that, in a similar vein to the adaptability of plants to various environments, it is highly probable for you to endure in practically any location. You will endure and persevere amidst an environment characterized by toxic elements. However, you shall not prosper. In a manner akin to certain plants that may grow yet fail to flourish outside their optimal conditions, you shall indeed navigate through life, but not achieve your utmost potential. To achieve optimal self-discovery, it is imperative to locate the suitable milieu that aligns with your true essence. It can be found in a certain location, albeit with the need for persistent effort in discovering its whereabouts.

www.ingramcontent.com/pod-product-compliance
Lightning Source LLC
Chambersburg PA
CBHW052146110526
44591CB00012B/1873